MEAN MACHINES

MONSTER TRUCKS

S A R A H   L E V E T E

Raintree

Chicago, Illinois

For information, address the publisher:
Raintree, 100 N. LaSalle, Suite 1200
Chicago, IL 60602
Customer Service: 888-363-4266
Visit our website at www.raintreelibrary.com

Printed and bound in China by South ChinaPrinting Company
09 08 07 06 05
10 9 8 7 6 5 4 3 2 1

Library of CongressCataloging-in-Publication Data
Levete, Sarah.
  Monster trucks / Sarah Levete.
    p. cm. -- (Mean machines)
  Includes bibliographical references and index.
  ISBN 1-4109-1082-2 (library binding - hardcover) -- ISBN 1-4109-1197-7
(pbk.) 1. Monster trucks--Juvenile literature. I. Title. II. Series.
  TL230.15.L48 2004
  629.224--dc22
                    2004015332

Acknowledgments
The publishers would like to thank the following for permission to reproduce photographs:
AATAC: p. 51; Bigge Crane and Rigging Company: pp. 50 (b), 54 (b); Bridgestone: pp. 5 (m), 12 (t); Corbis: pp. 5 (b) (Phillipa Lewis; Edifice), 17 (t) (Duomo), 19 (b) (Duomo), 29 (r) Minnesota Historical Society, 31 (b) (Bettmann), 35 (James L. Amos), 36 (t) (Phillipa Lewis; Edifice), 43 (r), 50 (t) (John H. Clark), 61 (Duomo); Ford: p. 16; Dennis Taft (www.monsterphotos.com): title page, pp. 5 (t), 13 (t), 16–17, 18, 19 (t), 20 (t), 21 (t), 22 (b), 22 (t), 23, 34 (b); Getty Images: pp. 4–5, 14 (b), 15 (Tim Defrisco), 20–21 (Tim Defrisco), 25 (Bill Greenblatt), 34 (t), 46 (t) (AFP); G M Media Archive: p. 31 (t); Hawaii Fire Department: p. 48; Hulton Archive: p. 30; Iveco (Tom Cunningham): pp. 37 (t), 44 (t), 44–45, 45, 60 (r); Kenworth: pp. 26–27; Klaus-Peter Kessler: p. 24 (t); MAN-Nutzfahrzeuge: p. 57 (t); NASA: pp. 38, 39; Neill Bruce Photography: pp. 28–29; Oshkosh Truck Corporation: pp. 47, 49 (b); Peter Bull: pp. 8 (b), 13, 28 (l); Peugeot: p. 56 (t); Scania: pp. 4 (b) (Dan Boman), 8 (Goran Wink), 11 (Dan Boman), 32 (Jonas Nordin), 33 (b) (Carl-Erik Andersson), 33 (t) (Ingemar Eriksson), 36–37 (Ingemar Eriksson), 41 (t) (Ingemar Eriksson), 43 (l) (Dan Boman), 49 (t) (Bryan Winstanley), 52 (t) (Jonas Nordin), 56 (b) (Johan Jonsson), 57 (b) (Goran Wink), 60 (l) (Goran Wink); Sparwood (www.sparwood.bc.ca): pp. 40–41; STRANA: p. 27 (b); TRH Pictures: pp. 24 (b), 46 (b); Volvo: pp. 6 (t), 6–7, 8 (t), 10, 11 (t), 12 (b), 42, 52 (b), 53, 54 (t), 55

Cover photograph of *Bigfoot* reproduced with permission of Actin Plus (Neale Haynes)

Every effort has been made to contact copyright holders of any material reproduced in this book. Any omissions will be rectified in subsequent printings if notice is given to the publishers.

The paper used to print this book comes from sustainable resources.

CONTENTS

Any words appearing in the text in bold, **like this,** are explained in the glossary. You can also look out for them in the "Up to Speed" box at the bottom of each page.

EXTREME MACHINES

Trucks rule the road. They carry the heaviest loads, from tons of gravel to missiles to whole houses. "Monster trucks" provide thrills at car shows as they crash into a line of parked cars. Other trucks are out on the road carrying race cars or moving tons of stone in a **quarry**. Other megamachines do the work no other trucks can handle.

TRUCKS AT WORK

The working trucks that carry loads across the world are sometimes called **big rigs**.

It takes a long time to get a monster truck like *Samson* looking so good and packed with so much power.

big rig   nickname for large truck carrying heavy loads

HANDLE WITH CARE

Many trucks gleam in the sunlight. Drivers polish the chrome lights and the sparkling paint. Other working trucks have no time for such loving care. These huge machines are built for power, not for looks.

It is not easy to handle twenty **gears** and twenty wheels and steer a huge piece of machinery around a tight corner. It takes skill to drive one of these trucks. Before you even get to the controls, you have to climb up to reach the driver's seat.

FIND OUT LATER . . .

Which **pickup truck** is the heaviest in the world?

What is the biggest tire ever used on a truck?

What is a **flatbed**?

gear one of two or more levels in a vehicle that control its direction and speed

5

TRUCK BASICS

It is easier for an articulated truck to turn around tight corners.

There are two basic types of truck: straight and **articulated.** Straight trucks are built on a single metal backbone called the **chassis,** pronounced "chass-ee." Other parts of the truck, such as the **cab,** engine, **axles,** and body, are attached to the chassis. The chassis is made from strong steel so it can support the truck's weight.

BENDING AROUND

Most huge trucks are articulated, meaning they consist of two parts. A tractor unit contains the powerful engine and the cab. The trailer, sometimes called the semitrailer, is the load-carrying part that is towed by the tractor unit. Articulated trucks bend in the middle, so they can drive around tight corners. The tractor and trailer can be separated.

exhaust

cab

suspension parts

brake drum

front axle

QUESTION

How can you steer a **big rig** with twenty wheels?

ANSWER

Have more pairs of wheels that turn in the direction of travel.

axle   connecting rod between pairs of wheels that allows them to turn

A COMFY RIDE

Thundering down a bumpy mountain road could damage a delicate load. It could also be very uncomfortable for the driver. **Suspensions** cushion the bumps in the road.

There are many types of suspensions. In most large trucks, air springs are fitted at the rear of the truck. When the truck hits a bump, the air in the springs is crushed. The springs then bounce back into shape. They—and not the driver—take the force of the bump. Metal springs are used in the front part of the truck.

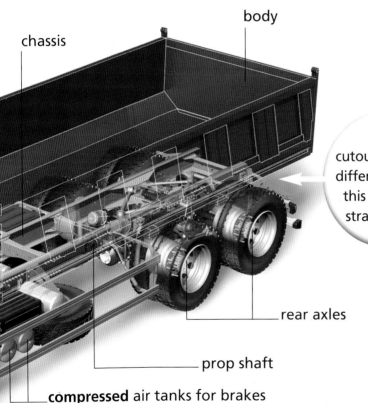

body

chassis

This cutout shows the different parts of this Volvo *FM9* straight truck.

rear axles

prop shaft

compressed air tanks for brakes

TURBO POWER

A turbocharger uses the **exhaust** gas flow from the engine to spin an air pump. This pushes more air into the cylinders. More fuel can be burned to increase the power.

air pump

exhaust turbine

POWER JUICE

Large trucks usually run on a fuel called diesel. Most diesel engines are **four-stroke** engines with four or more **cylinders**. A **piston** in each cylinder goes down and up, and down and up again. As the piston moves downward the first time, it sucks in fuel and air.

As it moves upward, the fuel and air mixture is **compressed** in a tiny space. This makes the mixture hot enough to explode. The energy from this explosion pushes the piston down and powers the truck. The final up-stroke pushes out the burned fuel gases.

The four-stroke cycle of an **overhead valve**, direct-injection diesel engine.

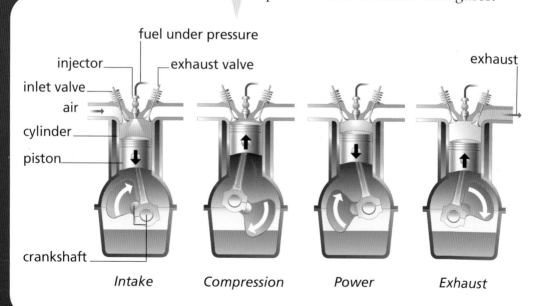

fuel under pressure

injector

inlet valve

air

cylinder

piston

exhaust valve

exhaust

crankshaft

Intake *Compression* *Power* *Exhaust*

piston   rod that fits in a cylinder and is moved by the pressure of liquid or gas

DECODE THE DETAIL

"16-liter turbocharged V8 direct injection diesel develops 645 hp and 1,947 lb ft at 1,900 rpm."

It helps to know what this technical information actually means:

- 16 liters: The volume of the cylinders.

- A turbocharger, or turbo, increases the engine's power.

- V8: The engine has two banks of four cylinders in a V shape.

- Direct injection: The diesel fuel goes directly into the cylinder to allow increased compression of air and fuel, which gives more power.

- Hp: This stands for **horsepower,** the modern measure of the maximum power of an engine.

- Pound foot: The measure used for a truck's **torque,** or pulling power.

- **Rpm**: Revolutions per minute. This is the speed at which the engine turns.

This is a brand-new, power-packed V8 16-liter engine made by Scania.

DID YOU KNOW?
An 18th-century **engineer** named James Watt used the amount of work done by horses in a mining pit to measure a machine's "horse power." Today, horse power is used to measure anything from scooters to **big rigs.**

A **big rig** may have up to twenty forward **gears** and four reverse gears. Due to its great weight, a rig needs many gears to help it get up to speed. A computerized system automatically figures out which gear is the most effective for any speed and weather conditions.

HAMMER DOWN

Megatrucks are designed to carry huge weights. It is amazing that they do more than crawl along when carrying their enormous loads. An average heavy load is 39 tons (35 metric tons). To compare, an adult male African elephant weighs about 6.6 tons (6 metric tons).

BIG BROTHER

A trucker may be alone in the truck, but others are watching. In some European countries, a device must be fitted to record the hours the driver works. Truckers must take breaks at set times to make sure they do not get too tired.

SHAPE IS ALL

Trucks with sharp corners and box shapes are old-fashioned. The smooth **aerodynamic** curves of modern trucks reduce **drag.** The engine does not waste energy battling against the wind.

Time/Distance   5/5

16:45   851km

23°C   03:12

0012156,5 KM

For more about driving safely, see page 55.

aerodynamic   has a smooth shape over which air can easily pass
cab   part of the vehicle where the driver and controls are located

STOP!

The weight of a load makes the rig zoom down a hill all too easily. Air brakes give the driver power to stop the truck quickly and safely. When the driver pushes the pedal, **compressed** air travels the length of the truck to the brake chambers at each wheel. The air pressure makes the brake shoes push against cast steel drums. The drums are attached to the wheels, and **friction** stops the truck. Sometimes brake pads are squeezed against steel discs. These are called disc brakes.

SATELLITES CAN HELP

A global positioning satellite (GPS) system in the **cab** can figure out the quickest route between two places. Using a screen, it can show the driver exactly where the truck is.

Wind passes easily over this truck's smooth, aerodynamic shape, allowing the driver to keep up speed.

---

drag   effect of air on a moving vehicle that slows it down
friction   slowing-down force of two surfaces rubbing against each other

CARRYING THE LOAD

Fitting a huge tire on a large truck can be a difficult and dangerous job. This is why tires are often fitted within a safety cage.

In some factories, special machines fit and **inflate** the tires for all the wheels that are **manufactured** there. It takes just twenty seconds to fit and inflate a tire.

RECORD BREAKER

The world's largest tire is 13 ft (396 cm) tall, 4.8 ft (147 cm) wide, and weighs 5.6 tons (5.1 metric tons). It was designed for 440-ton (400-metric-ton) dump trucks. The tire can support a load of 110 tons (100 metric tons).

ALL AIRED UP

The air pressure inside the tires holds all of the truck's weight. Higher air pressure can support heavier loads. Tire pressure that is too low causes trucks to use more fuel than necessary. This can also cause **blowouts**.

BLOWOUT

When a tire explodes, it can be very dangerous, especially at high speeds. The driver may struggle to keep control of the truck. Many big rigs do not carry spare tires because of the extra weight. The trucker must call a **mechanic** to replace the tire.

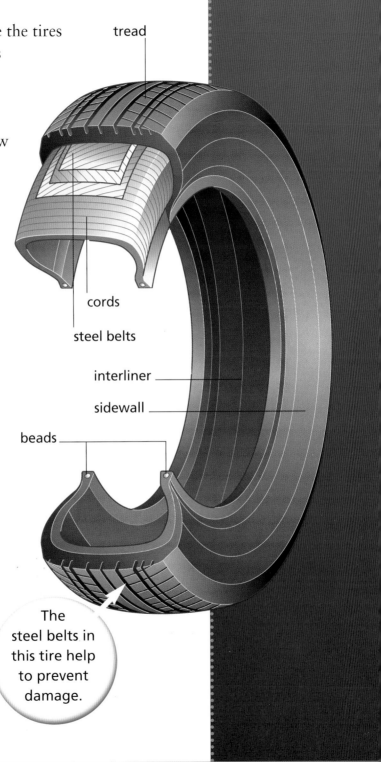

tread

cords

steel belts

interliner

sidewall

beads

The steel belts in this tire help to prevent damage.

MONSTER EVENTS

Competition and show trucks are special. To their owners, they are works of art and reflect the work of the world's best **engineers.**

MAKEOVER MAGIC

These incredible-looking machines are **customized.** Some are made from scratch. Others are built from regular **pickup trucks.** The owner buys a standard factory truck—but it does not stay ordinary for long. A new engine, changes to the body, and a lot of paint work the magic. You then have a "monster truck" with great looks and amazing power.

UPENDED

With its powerful 2,000 **horsepower** engine, a monster truck can easily rear up on its back wheels and perform a **wheelie.**

BIG AND MEAN

Unlike working trucks that travel long distances, these monster trucks are built for short bursts of speed. They break records and thrill crowds as they fly through the air. This is a sport for those who like their machines big and mean.

LIGHT AND STRONG

In the early days, monster trucks were made of metal. Now, they are made of lighter **fiberglass.** This is painted with great designs and **sponsors' logos.** The **chassis** is a frame of lightweight but strong steel tubes. The truck is covered by a steel structure called a roll cage. This protects the driver when the truck turns on its side or falls over backward after lifting up its front wheels.

The specially built, super-powerful engine is powered by methanol, an alcohol-based fuel. One monster truck can burn up to 2.5 gallons (9.5 liters) of methanol per run. A run is about 253 feet (77 meters).

NO DOORS

Monster trucks have a hole in the floor. Since there are no doors, the driver gets in through the hole in the floor! *Grave Digger,* pictured on page 22, is one of the few monsters to have doors.

DID YOU KNOW?

An average monster truck is 11 feet (3.4 meters) tall and 12 feet (3.6 meters) wide. To meet competition rules, it must not weigh less than 4.5 tons (4.1 metric tons). This is because a lighter truck can jump higher and move faster.

Forget doors! Strap yourself in. This truck is for jumping.

wheelie   riding a truck on its rear wheels with the front end lifted

HOW IT ALL BEGAN

A man named Bob Chandler wanted to promote his truck shop. He started to **customize** his Ford *F-250* **four-wheel drive pickup truck.** He added huge tires, an extreme **suspension,** and a more powerful engine. He named the truck *Bigfoot.*

Bob and *Bigfoot* started a new craze. The sport of monster trucks took off. In 1982 in Michigan, Bob and *Bigfoot* entered an event organized by the United States **Hot Rod** Association (USHRA).

RECORD BREAKER

Bigfoot holds several world records for the longest and highest outdoor monster truck jump and the longest monster truck **wheelie.**

It is hard to believe that the huge *Bigfoot 5* is built from this Ford *F-250.*

Weighing 14 tons (12.7 metric tons), *Bigfoot 5* is the world's largest and heaviest pickup truck.

customize   adjust to a specific design
fleet   several trucks

Driving one of these monsters takes skill and courage.

THE BIG TIME

Chandler and his Team Bigfoot are now big business. He and his **fleet** of monster trucks tour and compete in shows around the world.

ORGANIZING THE SPORT

Today, there are many organizations **promoting** monster truck events, from shows to competitions to monster festivals. The organizations make sure the trucks fit certain safety standards. The USHRA, the Monster Truck Racing Association (MTRA), and the European branch (MTRAE) all promote the sport.

SO YOU WANT TO JOIN IN THE FUN?

If you want to be a monster truck driver, you need to be at least 25 years old and have a commercial driving license. It also helps to be a **mechanic** or know about metalwork.

hot rod old vehicle stripped down and rebuilt for speed
promote advertise

More than 3,000 vehicles are crushed on purpose each year. And people pay to see the destruction.

At a car crush event, old buses, vans, and even airplanes are trashed as a monster truck slams into them. The bashed old vehicles come from scrap yards. They are returned there after the event even more battered!

Before the event, any glass is taken out of the wrecks. This protects the crowds from being hit by shattered glass.

ADDING UP THE COSTS

It is expensive to run a monster truck team. The trucks have to be taken to events in special trucks. Monsters guzzle up expensive fuel. After a crush or jump, each truck may need some repairs.

Monster trucks cannot be driven on public roads, so they are transported in huge trucks.

throttle   part that controls the amount of fuel that goes to the engine

READY TO GO?

Helmet on. Wait for the green light. Check the seat belts. Put your foot down and go! Charge toward the parked cars full **throttle**. Feel the **impact** as the truck lifts and then smashes down. Hear the crunch of the cars crumpling underneath the weight and force of the monster.

TIRES

At first, 4-foot (1.2-meter) diameter tractor tires were fitted on monster trucks. But soon, drivers wanted bigger tires. Today, monster truck tires are over 5.5 feet (1.7 meters) in diameter and are 3.5 feet (1.1 meters) wide. These tires are also often used on huge farm machinery.

Ford Motor Company and Marvel Comics **sponsor** some teams at USHRA Monster Jam events. Their sponsorship helps finance the truck and team. In return, they may ask for their **logo** to appear on advertising, posters, or even on the truck itself.

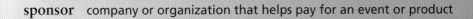

THE RACE IS ON

The first monster truck events featured trucks rolling over or smashing up other cars. Soon, the crowd was calling for more extreme thrills. To meet the demand, the trucks started to race against one another.

NITEMARE

The latest *Nitemare* truck features:

- Dodge *Ram* **fiberglass** body
- 557 Keith Black Hemi engine
- Firestone 5.5 ft (1.7 m) ×4.3 ft (1.3 m) tires
- Height 10.5 ft (3.2 m)
- Weight 4.7 tons (4.3 metric tons)

STYLES

Side-by-side racing involves two trucks racing alongside each other. In a freestyle race, drivers have a set time to show off their skills on the track. The fans are watching closely. They even get to choose the winning truck.

acceleration   ability to speed up
accelerator   foot pedal that controls the speed of the engine

TOUGH TALK

The word on the track is . . .

Burn out Spinning the truck's tires to get the mud off and gain **traction.**

Donut When a truck spins in circles in one spot.

Endo When a vehicle crashes and rolls end-over-end.

Drop the hammer To put the **accelerator** all the way down.

Stomp on it To jump on the accelerator.

Hammer The **throttle.**

Hook up To get enough traction for fast **acceleration.**

Hot shoe A good driver.

Mash the motor To accelerate.

Sky wheelie When a truck "stands" straight up, with the front tires in the air.

T-bone To crash head-on into the side of something.

STICKY GROUND

Tracks have to be laid and courses prepared for monster truck events. Some indoor tracks are made by covering the arena floor with soda drink syrup and a powder to dry it. This prevents the trucks from spinning wildly on the concrete floor.

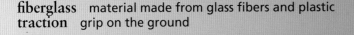

fiberglass   material made from glass fibers and plastic
traction   grip on the ground

NASTY NAMES

Bigfoot is not too scary a name. But what about *Grave Digger*, *Nitemare*, *Sudden Impact*, and *Maximum Destruction*? Truck names are meant to show the power and fierceness of both truck and driver.

LIFT AND BUMP

It is a thrill to drive through the air. But what happens to truck and driver when they hit the ground? Monster trucks need monster **suspensions** to cope with their high-flying stunts.

Grave Digger is up and flying.

impact   make contact forcefully

SUPER SUSPENSIONS

After jumping 98 feet (30 meters) through the air, *Grave Digger* needs a cushioned landing. The **shock absorbers** take most of the **impact.** They smooth out the bounces. Also, they allow an extra 2.2 feet (66 centimeters) of movement in the suspension for the wheels to bounce up and down.

Safety is very important at monster events, since the unexpected can happen.

FOUR-LINK

Some monster trucks have a four-link suspension. This is made up of four bars linking the front and rear **axles** to the frame. Drivers can adjust the suspension depending on how much ride height they need.

SAFETY

To protect the driver and crowd, there are strict safety standards. Drivers wear helmets, gloves, and fireproof suits. Each truck is fitted with strong seat belts and a fire extinguisher.

shock absorber   device that reduces the effect of sudden bumps and shocks

TOP TRUCKS

You may see the *M561 High Mobility Cargo Truck,* known as the *Gamma Goat* (below), rocking and rolling on a truck trial. It is named after its inventor, Roger Gamaunt, and a goat, because it handles rough, rocky ground like a goat can!

The British team driving the huge Tatra *813* in the Europa Truck Trials.

TO THE LIMIT

Truck trials are events that involve driving a large truck through a **quarry** or other very rough surfaces. They are not for the weakhearted. The aim is to finish the course. This is not easy when the ground is rough and full of obstacles. Trials are often timed and drivers have to beat the clock.

EUROPA TRUCK TRIALS

In this European competition, the rules are complicated and the competition is fierce. Drivers have to steer trucks between clearly marked gates without hitting the gates. The trial is not against the clock, so drivers can take their time.

FOUR-WHEEL DRIVE

There are many events for **four-wheel drive (4 x 4 or 4WD)** trucks. These are "off-road" vehicles, such as Jeeps and Land Rovers, and trucks you are likely to see on the roads called sport-utility vehicles (SUVs).

The engine in a 4WD turns all the wheels. With a two-wheel drive, only the front or rear wheels turn. 4WD gives the truck extra grip in slippery conditions or when the truck is pushed to the limit.

TUFF TRUCKS

"Tuff trucks" are small trucks such as **pickups.** They are allowed on roads, but their owners may have **customized** them with powerful engines and **suspensions.**

Magnus Ver Magnusson pulls a 30-ton (27-metric-ton) truck more than 69 ft (21 m).

HARD WORK!

Some people enjoy battling against trucks. In competitions, they test their strength in the strangest ways. They see if they can pull a truck!

pickup truck   open-bodied truck in which goods are placed
quarry   deep pit used for digging up stone and sand

The Pikes Peak
Hill Climb in
Colorado is a race
that starts at a
height of 9,488 ft
(2,892 m). The
12.4-mi (20-km)
gravel course
climbs to 14,245
ft (4,342 m).There
are 156 turns as
well as drops of
2,018 ft (615 m)
with no guard
rails. Winning
times are under
fourteen minutes.

PROFESSIONAL RACING

Some trucks just race. They are made for speed.
Drivers in truck racing are usually part of a large
team of **mechanics** and designers organized by
the maker of the truck. **State-of-the-art** engines,
suspensions, and designs give the truck a racing
edge. There are separate truck races for people to
enter their own trucks.

Inside each **cab** is a roll cage. This will protect
the driver in case of a high-speed
crash. Racing seats are fitted
into each cab.

This Kenworth
T2000 takes part
in the demanding
2003 Pikes Peak
challenge.

BRUCE CANEPA

www.kenworth.com

BRIDGESTONE

KENWORTH

COMPUTER TECH

Some cabs are fitted with the latest in hi-tech computer controls. **Sensors** fitted to different parts of the truck display information on a screen about:

- speed
- engine **rpm**
- **lap** time and lap number
- water temperature.

TECH TALK

Kenworth T2000 Pikes Peak Special
- Twin turbo, 6-cylinder 18-liter engine
- 1,375 **hp** at 10,095 ft (3,077 m) height
- 5.4 tons (4.9 metric tons)
- Hand-cut tires on rear-drive wheels

TUNED UP

The Super Truck Racing Association of North America (STRANA) uses trucks built just for racing. Teams can use one of several approved engines. They make changes to give a truck its own style and power features.

This Tonka was built for the STRANA race.

TRUCKING DAYS

Until the middle of the 18th century, horses pulled carts. These were the first vehicles to carry goods or passengers. In 1769 Nicholas Cugnot designed the first steam truck. This truck could travel at 3 miles (5 kilometers) per hour, but only for fifteen minutes. Solid wooden tires made the ride very uncomfortable.

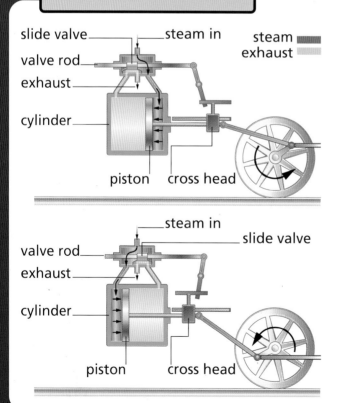

slide valve — steam in
valve rod
exhaust
cylinder
piston   cross head

steam
exhaust

valve rod — steam in — slide valve
exhaust
cylinder
piston   cross head

MORRIS'S
SHREWSBURY

KF 6482

FULL STEAM AHEAD!

In 1892 Maurice LeBlanc produced a small steam-powered truck. It went at about 4 miles (6.4 kilometers) per hour, or about the same speed as walking very quickly.

Soon, the thick black smoke from steam engines was a thing of the past. Better engines that burned **petroleum** oils were invented.

In 1876 a German **engineer** named Nikolaus Otto developed an engine using a **four-stroke cycle.** He combined this with the use of more than one **cylinder** to make it run more smoothly.

OUTSIDE OR IN?

In a steam engine, the fuel (coal) is burned outside the engine. In the engine designed by a French engineer, Etienne Lenoir, the fuel is burned inside the engine. This is why it is called an internal **combustion** engine.

A 1931 Sentinel steam truck showing the steam boiler, chimney, and steam **exhaust.**

This 1903 traction engine is driven over a block to show the power of steam.

◄◄◄◄◄◄◄◄◄
For more on the four-stroke engine, see page 8.

petroleum   oil found naturally in Earth's crust. Gasoline comes from it.

The driver had to turn a starting handle on this Leyland truck.

LEYLAND

In 1896 the first vehicle produced by the Lancashire Steam Motor Company in Leyland, England, was a steam truck that could support 1.2 tons (1.1 metric tons). Leyland now employs 1,000 people and **manufactures** 14,000 trucks a year.

GETTING BETTER

In the early 20th century, the Lacre Motor Car Company began to **manufacture** motor cars and vans. These vans had simple **suspensions** and electric lights. **Pneumatic** tires replaced the hard, solid tires. An enclosed **cab** kept the driver dry and more comfortable. Traveling was improving!

NEW DEVELOPMENTS

1915 The first separate tractor and trailer units were designed by an American blacksmith named August Fruehauf.

1929 Chevrolet's **overhead valve**, 6-cylinder engine with a volume of 194 cubic inches and 46 **horsepower** was a first for the light-truck industry.

1950 The addition of turbochargers upped the power of trucks by a huge 50 percent.

1951 Chrysler's power steering directed the wheels on two front **axles** instead of one. This made it possible to steer heavier trucks.

1955 Chevrolet produced a V8 engine of 265 cubic inches and 132 horsepower.

horsepower   measure of an engine's maximum power
manufacture   make or produce

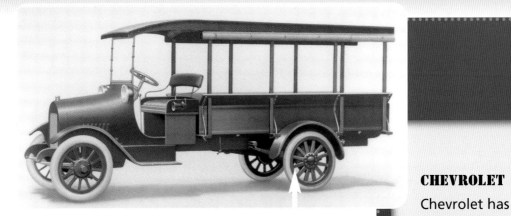

DIESEL POWER

In 1892 Rudolf Diesel invented the diesel engine for ships and trains. Later, this was used in trucks and heavy vehicles. It is a hard-wearing engine that uses up less fuel than a petroleum engine (an engine that uses gasoline).

Truck design has improved since the early days.

WAR TRUCKING

During World War I (1914–18), trucks were used to transport troops and weapons across Europe and the United States. This was the first time that trucks had been used so widely.

CHEVROLET

Chevrolet has been building and designing trucks for nearly 100 years. The first Chevrolet, or Chevy, was built in 1918.

In World War I, soldiers were taken to battle in **convoys** of trucks.

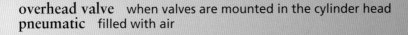

overhead valve   when valves are mounted in the cylinder head
pneumatic   filled with air

BUILDING A TRUCK

Huge trucks are built to last. With complex engines and specific details for each type of load, it takes months to design and build a truck.

A truck is first designed by **engineers** and designers on a computer. This is called computer-aided design (CAD). New truck designs are closely guarded secrets. Trucks that are better, bigger, and faster than anyone else's can mean huge success for a company.

AN INTERNATIONAL APPROACH

Huge amounts of materials are used to make a truck, from **fiberglass**, aluminum, and steel for the body to shatterproof glass for the windshield. Every part of the truck needs the best materials. These may come from all over the world.

MANY MANUFACTURERS

Some of the truck designers and manufacturers popular around the world today have been working for around 100 years.

Chrysler • DAF • Chevrolet • Ford • Leyland • MAN Scania • Iveco

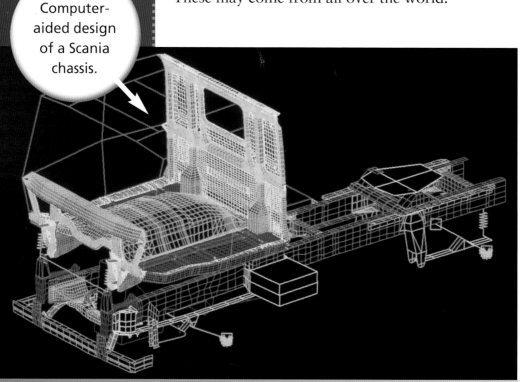

Computer-aided design of a Scania chassis.

FIRST TRY

Before a truck is sold to customers, a **prototype** is made. The company can then examine its performance and safety and make any changes. When they are satisfied, the truck can be **manufactured**.

WHO'S WHO

Designers and engineers They create new ideas for improved performance.

Mechanics They assemble the truck parts from the **chassis** to the engine.

The production manager He or she manages the team making the parts.

Safety inspectors They check to make sure the truck meets strict safety measures.

The sales team They advertise and sell the trucks.

A weight of 1.6 tons (1.5 metric tons) is dropped onto the **cab** to test how it stands up to **impact**.

TESTING, TESTING, TESTING

Trucks are crashed and crashed again. A team of experts tests the strength of the truck in case of an accident to figure out how much protection the driver has. Instead of a driver, a dummy sits in the driver's seat.

A truck starts life as a computer design. After a long process, it is produced in a factory.

33

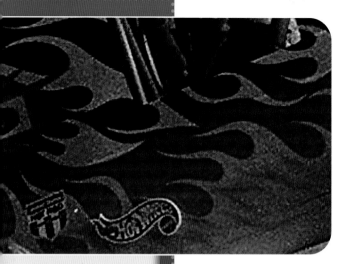

MAKING A MONSTER TRUCK

What is special about building a monster truck?

It can take from three months to one year to build one from scratch.

It takes longer than **customizing** a factory-model truck.

LOOKING GOOD

The truck's power must be matched by dramatic looks. Faces, monsters, wings, and flames are just some of the pictures seen on a monster truck. It takes more than a splash of paint to make these machines look so mean.

Some pieces, such as the **chassis,** are custom-made. A specialist company often makes the body. The tires are designed for another use, but they are adapted to monster needs. A team will put together all the parts before painting it.

This amazing **suspension** belongs to the monster truck *Predator.*

chassis   strong metal framework on which a vehicle is built
ventilation   air flow

WOULD YOU BELIEVE?

Because monster truck tires are not made specially, it takes 50 hours to prepare a tire. The tread of each tire is cut by hand. This gives the truck more **traction** and removes weight by an incredible 450 pounds (204 kilograms) for each cut tire. Before cutting, the tire weighs approximately 880 pounds (400 kilograms).

LIGHT BUT HARD

If a truck is too heavy, it will not be able to jump or get up a good speed. But it needs to be strong enough to survive huge **impacts** from landings and crushes. Designers are constantly looking for improved materials to perfect the monster machine.

Special car paint is used for monster trucks. It is hard-wearing but gives off dangerous fumes. The truck is painted in a room with plenty of **ventilation**. The floor is kept wet to stop floor dust from sticking to the wet paint.

TRUCKS AT WORK

We have seen monster trucks at play. But what about the trucks that do real work? These working trucks pull the heaviest loads, travel down the steepest roads, and work in the most difficult places to reach.

Only the meanest machines can get into forests, down **quarries,** and even across rivers.

MOVING

A flatbed truck can carry a house. The house is loaded onto the truck and driven to a new location. It is then unloaded, and the owners have the same house, just in a different area.

convoy   large group of trucks traveling together
flatbed   truck with a flat cargo area

TRUCK POWER

Truckers know the power they have—and not just engine power. Trucks are powerful in other ways. A long line, or **convoy,** of trucks can block a road and cause huge traffic jams. If truckers decide not to work, goods are not delivered, which could mean no fuel at gas stations and no food in the stores.

BUILD A ROAD AND LOAD!

In the remote logging areas of Alaska, there are no roads for trucks. So roads have to be built first. Crushed rock and gravel form these roads.

Special trucks scoop up bundles of logs and put them onto **flatbed** trucks. Each bundle can weigh more than 22 tons (20 metric tons).

TRUCK LOAD

Some trucks even carry other trucks. This Iveco transporter takes a Caterpillar truck to and from the building site or quarry.

This flatbed truck can carry a load of 80 tons (73 metric tons).

THE ROAD TO SPACE

People gasp and gaze at space rockets blasting off. But do they know how the rockets reach their launch destination?

The *Marion Crawler* takes rockets and space shuttles to the Kennedy Space Center launchpad. This is no ordinary truck. It makes any **big rig** look like a toy in comparison.

IN THE MAKING

The *Marion Crawlers* were designed by a team of **engineers** at the Kennedy Space Center. The team decided to build a Saturn V rocket in a vehicle assembly building (VAB) and then transport it fully assembled on one of the *Marion Crawlers* to the launchpad.

TECH TALK

Largest tracked vehicle
Each eight-tracked *Marion Crawler:*

- is 131 ft (40 m) long and 115 ft (35 m) wide;
- consists of four double-tracked crawlers, each 10 ft (3 m) high and 39 ft (12 m) long;
- has a flat, square top **deck** about 89 ft (27 m) long on each side.

Each 3,000-ton (2,700-metric-ton) crawler can carry a 6,000-ton (5,400-metric-ton) Saturn V rocket several miles. The rocket has to be kept upright without leaning more than about 3 in. (8 cm). The crawler is fitted with devices to keep the rocket stable. It is built for strength, not speed.

Since 1977 the *Marion Crawlers* have traveled an amazing 1,234 miles (1,986 kilometers). About twenty trips like this could take you around the world.

The crawler's maximum speed is 1 mi (1.6 km) per hour.

SLOW BUT SURE

The crawler rides on four double tracks, each pair the size of a bus. Inside its huge deck are diesel engines of about 8,000 **horsepower.** The engines drive generators that power electric motors for the tracks. The crawler burns 150 gallons of diesel oil per mile (353 liters every 1000 meters).

DUMP IT!

Some of the most amazing megamachines are dump trucks. They work in **quarries** and mines and on large building projects.

A fully loaded giant dump truck can weigh an incredible 551 tons (500 metric tons) and have a 2,700-**horsepower** engine. Its tank can hold 1,201 gallons (4,548 liters) of fuel. Each tire costs about $25,000!

Imagine a bucket as big as a building. Now, take a look at this picture of the *Terex Titan*, **manufactured** by General Motors of Canada. This is still one of the world's largest dump trucks. It can hold a huge 349-ton (317-metric-ton) load in its **hopper.**

PUTTING IT TOGETHER

In 1978 the *Titan* was brought to work in pieces on a train! It traveled about 1,000 miles (1,610 kilometers) from California to a mine in Sparwood, Canada. Upon arrival, *Titan* was put together.

CHECK IT OUT

Terex Titan Facts
- Weight: 260 tons (236 metric tons)
- Maximum load: 349 tons (317 metric tons)
- Tire diameter: 11 ft (338 cm)
- Tire weight: 4 tons (3.6 metric tons)
- Fuel tank: holds 800 gallons (3,028 liters) of fuel

generator   machine that produces electric energy
hopper   huge bucket holding materials such as rock or grain

TITANIC

The *Titan* is powered by a 16-**cylinder**, 3,300-horsepower **locomotive** engine. The engine is used with a **generator** to deliver power to four **traction** motors located on the rear wheels. The generator is powerful enough to supply electricity to 250 modern homes.

TECH TALK

The back of a dump truck is raised by a **hydraulic** ram. This is a **piston** that is forced along a tube by oil pressure. It is powered by the truck's engine.

SPARWOOD B.C.

The Terex Titan is one of the largest trucks in the world.

ON THE ROAD

In the Australian outback, there are no railroads. Roads are narrow. The heat is intense. Extremely long trucks **haul** huge loads over long distances. They consist of a tractor unit and several trailers hooked together.

PULLING POWER

A standard truck in the outback is made up of three 44-foot (13.5-meter) trailers. The 450-**horsepower** engine is pulling 131 feet (40 meters) of truck. A twin steering **axle** under the front of one trailer is hooked up to the back of the trailer in front of it with solid metal bars.

The typical load of a three-trailer truck is 132 tons (120 metric tons).

DRY AND DUSTY

Conditions in the outback are harsh. Drivers often journey at night to keep cool. Searing heat and dusty roads test trucks to the limit. Special air filters protect the engine from the dry dust.

WATCH THE ROO!

One of the dangers of the road is kangaroos. They may hop in front of the speeding truck. A thick metal grill called a roo guard or bull bar protects the truck, but there is little to protect the kangaroos from the truck. Let's hope they stay off the road.

REPAIRS

A truck driver can drive for hundreds of miles before seeing another person in the outback. If the truck has a serious problem, a traveling **mechanic** may not be able to fix it. The truck will have to be towed to the next service station.

EARLY LONG TRUCKS

The first long trucks in the 1940s used old U.S. Army trucks. There were no brakes, so in order to stop, the driver just took his foot off the **accelerator!**

This roo guard protects the speeding truck if it hits a kangaroo.

> > > > > > > > > > > >
For more about life on the road, see pages 52–53.

RACE ACTION

Auto racing circuits are busy with **engineers, mechanics,** drivers, and **state-of-the-art** racing cars. The cars are not driven to races on the roads. They are taken there in specially equipped trucks called race transporters.

A race transporter is not just a truck. It is a garage, a chill-out room, and more!

WHEELS WITHIN WHEELS

The transporter has plenty of room inside for four cars. The upper **deck** holds this Ferrari *F1* racing car and a race-ready extra car. On the lower deck are another racing car and an extra **chassis.**

engineer   person who uses science to design and build machines

HOME FROM HOME

In addition to taking care of the cars, there is plenty of space in the truck for the team and drivers. A meeting room, work space, and sitting area provide some home comforts. Here, the team can plan details of the race. The truck is equipped with computers and televisions. A kitchen with a refrigerator full of tasty snacks makes the journey more pleasant for all.

The huge Iveco Stralis transports the Scuderia Ferrari Formula One team to the Grand Prix races.

SIDE-BY-SIDE

At the race circuit, these two transporters park next to each other. They have to be in position to the inch. Huge **hydraulic** rams then lift a second floor of office space, including two staircases, onto the trailers of the two vehicles.

The tough 7,000-mile (11,200-kilometer) off-road trek called the Paris–Dakar Rally takes vehicles through icy conditions, mountains, and hot deserts.

DESERT TRUCKS

Trucks need extra cooling systems in extreme heat. They have very large fuel tanks so that they do not run out of gas in the desert. The rough, bumpy ground bounces the truck around, so they need strong **suspensions**.

AMPHIBIOUS TRUCKS

Some trucks are designed for both land and water. These are called **amphibious** trucks. Armies often use them to transport troops and weapons across small rivers. Some people use them as an unusual way to get around and have fun.

The *Pandur* drives through water.

amphibious   can be used on land and in water
hull   body of a boat

This truck can deal with heavy snowfall.

GETTING WET

The *Pandur* is an amphibious six-wheel drive armored vehicle. The engine powers both wheels on land and a **propeller** under water. It has an extended **exhaust** pipe and water jets on the back of the **hull**. It can "swim" at a maximum speed of 6.8 miles (11 kilometers) per hour. In just eight seconds, the truck can turn around to face the opposite direction in the water.

SNOW TRUCKS

Snow trucks are designed to stay stable in icy conditions. Extra wide wheels give them greater **traction**. Some trucks, such as the Oshkosh H series snowplow, can move 1.1 tons (1 metric ton) of snow per second.

propeller   part with blades that turns to push a boat through water

PUT IT OUT

Water, foam, ladders, heavy tools, elevators—
these are just a few pieces of equipment needed
to deal with raging fires. To reach a fire, the
truck needs to be fast and reliable. Combining a
large, well-equipped truck with the speed and
smoothness of a sports car is quite a challenge.

EARLY FIRE ENGINES

The first fire engines were powered by steam and
horses. A steam-driven water pump provided
water to put out the flames. The 1901 fire
engine, called *Firefly*, was pulled by horses.
Before the firefighters could get to the fire, they
had to **harness** the horses to the wagon and light
the fire in the boiler!

DIFFERENT MACHINE, DIFFERENT USE

There are many types of fire trucks, used for different purposes. Many carry tanks of water on board and hold foam to deal with oil and chemical fires. Some fire trucks have a long arm called a boom. This can reach the highest places. Special legs called jacks keep the truck steady when the boom or ladder is extended.

DANGEROUS WORK

Exploding fuel is the main danger in this aircraft fire. The crews pump foam to put out the blaze. The foam blankets the burning fuel by keeping the air out. This stops the fuel from burning.

The long boom sprays out water or foam, reaching close to the raging flames.

WEIRD LOADS

Trucks are often made to deal with very heavy and unusual loads.

A huge mining machine called a dragline was moved from a coal mine in Centralia, Washington. To do this, a transporter was built that was made up of 24 **modules.** Each module is like a platform, about 8 feet (2.5 meters) wide. Each has four or five **axles,** and each axle has four tires. Six of the modules are equipped with a diesel engine, packed with 500 **horsepower.** These power the **hydraulic** drive system.

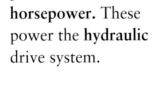

AIRPORT TUG

Airplanes can fly. But they cannot drive along at slow speeds without starting their noisy engines. This rather small-looking truck is powerful enough to pull aircraft short distances on the ground. The aircraft "tug" fits snugly under the airplane's nose.

This transporter has 432 wheels.

STEER

Imagine trying to steer 432 wheels with only 6 inches (15 centimeters) of space between your truck and a bridge. Instead of stressing out a driver, a computer took charge of the steering. It figured out the correct position of each wheel as the transporter moved.

The combined weight of the load and the transporter was an incredible 4,200 tons (3,810 metric tons). Tires similar to those on a dump truck supported this weight.

IT'S A WINNER!

Shaughnessy & Company, the company that succeeded in moving the enormous machine, won the Specialized Carriers & Riggers Association 1998 "Haul of the Year" award.

RECOVERY TRUCK

To move a truck that has broken down, another huge machine is brought to work. With **hydraulic** lifting equipment, **winches,** and steel cables, the recovery truck can lift the heaviest of trucks.

◄ ◄ ◄ ◄ ◄ ◄ ◄ ◄ ◄ ◄
For more about tires, see pages 12–13.

winch   rotating reel that winds up a cable

THE TRUCKER'S LIFE

A trucker's life is hard. The driver needs to feel comfortable and relaxed, even after hours on the road. Some **cabs** have a built-in sleeping area and a mini-kitchen with a refrigerator and microwave. Some are fitted with televisions and computers. But these are only for use when not driving!

Even drivers need to take a break.

A computer watches what is going on in the engine. A screen in the cab shows the driver what is happening. If something is wrong— for example, the oil level is low or the temperature too high—the computer screen will flash a warning.

A truck driver needs comfort and space in the cab.

FRIENDLY TALK

CB radio is a trucker's friend. CB stands for "citizens' band." Other drivers tune their radios to the CB wavelength. The truckers can then "talk" to each other. They often give themselves nicknames such as Blue Bob or Rubber Duck.

You may need a phrase book to understand truckers on CB radio. These are just a few of the phrases they use:

Over I have finished my transmission and you may speak when ready.

Hammer down Driving fast.

Dead pedal Slow car or truck.

Do you copy? Do you understand?

Roger Yes, or OK.

Ten-four OK, or message received.

WHAT DOES IT TAKE TO BE A TRUCKER?

To gain a commercial driving license, a new driver needs to go to driving school. Here, the learner drives in a **simulator.** Video clips show what to do and what not to do in difficult situations.

Special courses give a driver skill in handling dangerous loads. These may be chemicals or very long loads, such as triple trailers.

Written exams and driving skills tests ensure that the driver is able to handle heavy vehicles.

It takes skill to drive a machine as mean and huge as this one.

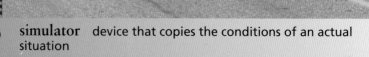

simulator   device that copies the conditions of an actual situation

Truck drivers may have to drive in very difficult conditions.

SAFETY TIPS

- Inspect the truck—check the tires, wipers, and fluid levels.
- Do not drive when tired, upset, or sick.
- Keep to the speed limit.
- Drive with headlights on in rain, fog, snow, at dusk, and at dawn.
- Slow down at night and in poor weather conditions.
- Keep a good distance between you and the vehicle in front.
- Never use a phone while driving.
- Expect the unexpected.

TRUE OR FALSE?

Keep your eyes looking straight in front at all times.

Answer: False
You need to keep your eyes looking around the road and in your mirrors.

TRUCK TALK

Truckers have their own language:
Dragon wagon Tow truck
Flip flop Trucker's return trip
Going horizontal Going to sleep
Shiny side Top of the trailer

55

TRUCKS OF THE FUTURE

Designers and **engineers** continue to work on improved designs to make trucks cleaner, quieter, and safer. These ideas are often developed into a **prototype** or **concept truck** to see if the designs are working.

There are three areas that designers are working on:

- cheaper, cleaner fuels
- ways to make trucks lighter
- experiments to make trucks more **aerodynamic.**

H²O

The Peugeot H^2O is a concept vehicle that is driven by hydrogen. It is an environmentally friendly fire engine.

This future Scania tractor unit is first designed on paper.

ELECTRIC TRUCK

One way to create trucks that are more **environmentally friendly** is to use electricity in addition to ordinary fuel.

A prototype electric truck has been produced that runs on either diesel or electricity. The **hybrid** electric vehicle drastically cuts down on the **pollution** created by diesel engines. The truck is quiet, smooth, and fast.

FUEL CELLS

The fuel cell is being developed. It uses hydrogen combining with oxygen to produce electricity very cleanly. Water is the only waste product.

In the future, we are likely to see lighter, more aerodynamic trucks that burn hydrogen. They will have a smoother shape, more like the body of an airplane.

This designer is working on a clay model of a future MAN cab.

MATERIAL WORLD

Materials such as aluminum and reinforced plastics will make this Scania concept truck lighter. This will cut down on the amount of fuel the truck uses.

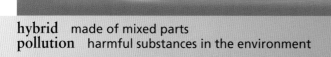

hybrid   made of mixed parts
pollution   harmful substances in the environment

TRUCK FACTS

EUROPEAN SUPER TRUCK RACING CHAMPIONS

Year	Driver	Truck	Country
2003	Gerd Körber	Buggyra MK002	Germany
2002	Gerd Körber	Buggyra MK002	Germany
2001	Stan Matejovsky	Tatra	Czech Republic
2000	Harri Luostarinen	Caterpillar-TRD	Finland
1999	Fritz Kreutzpointer	MAN	Germany
1998	Ludovic Faure	Mercedes-Benz	France
1997	Harri Luostarinen	Caterpillar-TRD	Finland

MONSTER JAM WORLD FINALS: RACING

Year	Driver	Truck	Country
2004	Dennis Anderson	Grave Digger	United States
2003	Brian Barthel	Wolverine	United States
2002	Tom Meents	Goldberg	United States

MONSTER JAM WORLD FINALS: FREESTYLE

Year	Driver	Truck	Country
2004	(tie) Andrew Porter	Maximum Destruction	United States
	Lupe Sosa	El Toro Loco	
2003	Jim Koehler	Avenger	United States
2002	Tom Meents	Goldberg	United States

Dorian Lugo has been a truck driver for fifteen years. She has driven 1 million miles (1,630,542 kilometers) without an accident.

WORLD'S FASTEST SUPER RACE TRUCK DRIVER

Year	Driver	Truck	Speed	Country
2004	David Vrsecky	Buggyra	174.94 mph 281.723 km/h	Czech Republic

WORLD'S FASTEST PRODUCTION PICKUP TRUCK

Year	Driver	Truck	Speed	Country
2004	Brendan Gaughan	Dodge Ram SRT-10	154.587 mph 248.783 km/h	United States

WORLD'S HIGHEST MONSTER TRUCK JUMP OVER A 727 JET AIRLINER

Year	Driver	Truck	Height	Distance
1999	Dan Runte	Bigfoot 14	23.8 ft (7.24 m)	203 ft (62 m)

WORLD'S FASTEST MONSTER TRUCK IN COMPETITION

Year	Driver	Truck	Speed	Distance
1996	Fred Shafer	Bear Foot	4.59 sec	300 ft (91.5 m)

Molly Morter won "Rookie of the Year" in the 2002 Pikes Peak Hill Climb.

A 2-mile (3.2-kilometer) **convoy** of 14 trucks and 21 ambulances carried 551 tons (500 metric tons) of supplies from Clonmel, Ireland, to the nuclear-affected region of Chernobyl, Ukraine, in 2002. The convoy traveled 3,000 miles (4,830 kilometers) through ten European countries.

FIND OUT MORE

ORGANIZATIONS

**International Motor
Sports Association**

1394 Broadway Avenue

Braselton, Georgia 30517

info@imsaracing.net

**Monster Truck Racing
Association (MTRA)**

14843 April Drive

Loxahatchee, FL 33470

mtramembership@
adelphia.net

**United States Hot Rod
Association (USHRA)**

495 N. Commons Drive

Suite 200

Aurora, IL 60504

webmaster@ushra.com

BOOKS

Bolognese, Don. *Monster Truck Demolition Derby!* Minneapolis, Minn.: Sagebrush Education, 2001.

Graham, Ian. *Super Trucks.* Danbury, Conn.: Scholastic Library, 2001.

Johnstone, Michael. *Monster Trucks.* Minneapolis, Minn.: Lerner Publishing, 2001.

Tieck, Sarah. *Monster Trucks.* Edina, Minn.: ABDO Publishing, 2005.

WORLD WIDE WEB

If you want to find out more about extreme trucks, you can search the Internet using keywords like these:

- monster truck
- **four-wheel drive**
- **big rig**
- truck racing
- truck trial
- **hybrid** trucks

Make your own keywords using headings or words from this book. The search tips on the next page will help you to find the most useful websites.

SEARCH TIPS

There are billions of pages on the Internet, so it can be difficult to find exactly what you want to find. If you just type in "truck" on a search engine such as Google, you will get a list of millions of web pages. These search skills will help you find useful websites more quickly:

- Use simple keywords, not whole sentences.
- Use two to six keywords in a search.
- Be precise—only use names of people, places, or things.
- If you want to find words that go together, put quote marks around them—for example "world speed record."
- Use the advanced section of your search engine.
- Use the "+" sign between keywords to find pages with all these words.

WHERE TO SEARCH

SEARCH ENGINE

Each search engine looks through millions of web pages and lists all sites that match the search words. The best matches are at the top of the list, on the first page. Try **google.com**.

SEARCH DIRECTORY

A search directory is like a library of websites. You can search by keyword or subject and browse through the different sites as you would look through books on a library shelf. A good example is **yahooligans.com**.

GLOSSARY

acceleration ability to speed up

accelerator foot pedal that controls the speed of the engine

aerodynamic has a smooth shape over which air can easily pass

amphibious able to be used on both land and water

articulated having two connected parts that bend in the middle

axle connecting rod between pairs of wheels that allows them to turn

big rig nickname for large truck carrying heavy loads

blowout when a tire explodes

cab part of vehicle where the driver and controls are located

chassis strong metal framework on which a vehicle is built

combustion burning of fuel and air to produce energy

compressed crushed or squeezed

concept truck type of truck that features the newest design

convoy large group of trucks traveling together

customize adjust to a specific design

cylinder piston chamber in an engine

deck floor or level

drag effect of air on a moving vehicle that slows it down

engineer person who uses science to design and build machines

environmentally friendly does little harm to the natural world

exhaust waste gas from an engine

fiberglass material made from glass fibers and plastic

flatbed truck with a flat cargo area

fleet several trucks

four-stroke cycle engine in which each cycle requires four strokes of the piston

four-wheel drive (4×4, 4WD) when all four wheels are turned directly by the engine

friction slowing-down force of two surfaces rubbing against each other

gear one of two or more levels in a vehicle that control its direction and speed

generator machine that produces electric energy

harness attach

haul pull

hopper huge bucket holding materials such as rock or grain

horsepower measurement of the maximum power of an engine

hot rod old vehicle stripped down and rebuilt for speed

hull body of a boat

hybrid made of mixed parts

hydraulic moved by liquid under pressure

impact make contact forcefully

inflate fill with air

lap one complete round of a course

locomotive railroad vehicle used for pulling trains

logo image or design representing a company

manufacture make or produce

mechanic person who knows how to repair and build vehicles

module standard part

overhead valve when valves are mounted in the cylinder head

petroleum oil found naturally in Earth's crust. Gasoline comes from it.

pickup truck open-bodied truck in which goods can be placed

piston rod that fits in a cylinder and is moved by the pressure of liquid or gas

pneumatic filled with air

pollution harmful substances in the environment

promote advertise

propeller part with blades that turns to push a boat through water

prototype first model used to test the success of the design

quarry deep pit used for digging up stone and sand

rpm (revolutions per minute) speed at which an engine turns

sensor electronic device that notices something and alerts the driver

shock absorber device that reduces the effect of sudden bumps and shocks

simulator device that copies the conditions of an actual situation

sponsor company or organization that helps pay for an event or product

state of the art reaching the highest levels of development at the time

suspension system of air or metal springs that cushion the vehicle and driver from bumps in the road

throttle part that controls the amount of fuel that goes to the engine

torque twisting action on the shaft that runs from the engine to the axle to the wheel

traction grip on the ground

ventilation air flow

wheelie riding a truck on its rear wheels with the front end lifted

winch rotating reel that winds up a cable

INDEX